Other Books by Mark Fleckenstein

Making Up the World (Editions Dedicaces, 2018)
God Box (Clare Songbird Publishing, 2019)
Lowercase God (Unsolicited Press, 2022)

Chapbooks

The Memory of Stars (Sticks Press, 1995)
I Was I, Drowning Knee Deep (Sticks Press, 2007)
Memoir as Conversation (Unsolicited Press, 2019)

A Name for Everything

Mark Fleckenstein

Červená Barva Press
Somerville, Massachusetts

Červená Barva Press
P.O. Box 440357
W. Somerville, MA 02144-3222

www.cervenabarvapress.com

Bookstore: www.thelostbookshelf.com

Cover Art: Mark Fleckenstein

Cover Design: William J. Kelle

ISBN: 978-1-950063-04-8

Library of Congress Control Number: 2019954408

ACKNOWLEDGMENTS

Grateful acknowledgement to the editors of The Little Magazine, BL(u)R, Istanbul Literary Review and Sticks Press where several of these poems (often radically different versions) first appeared.

Several poems in *Failed Stars* first appeared in *I Am I, Drowning Knee Deep*, an online chapbook by Stick Press.

The Memory Of Stars was first published by Sticks Press as a chapbook.

Special thanks and severe appreciation to Gloria Mindock, for years of friendship, support, her keen editorial eye and great poems, and the late Mary Veazey, for publishing several of these poems, and whose gentle suggestions that saved many others.

TABLE OF CONTENTS

I. ALWAYS BEGIN WHERE YOU ARE

ALWAYS BEGIN WHERE YOU ARE 3
SIN EATING 4
CARTOGRAPHY 5
THE MEMORY OF STARS 6
A DESCRIPTIVE HISTORY OF MEMORY 10
A NAME FOR EVERYTHING 17

II. FALLEN STARS

LOOKING FOR FALLING STARS, JULY 2006 21
DREAMING IN FLESH, OF FLESH 22
SELF PORTRAIT WITH COFFEE 23
CONTEMPLATIVE, CURIOUS, THE BODY 24
STUDY FOR FOUR HANDS 25
PRAYER IN THE RAIN 26
WEATHER REPORT 27
A LOVELY QUICKNESS 28
NOCTOURNE 29
MUSIC OF BROKEN LIGHTS 30
AN APOLOGY FROM ANOTHER SIDE OF THE 31
    OCEAN
LETTER TO TRIESTE 32

III. LETTERS RESCUED FROM A FIRE

SLOWDANCING WITH THE WOMAN IN RED 35
    SHOES
PLAYING HOUSE36
DESIRE 37
PARABLE 38
VALENTINE 39
PRESENT 40
EVE OF SPRING 41
BETWEEN FACT AND TRUTH 42
ALWAYS BEGIN WHERE YOU ARE 43
STILL LIFE WITH DEAD BIRDS 44

OCCASION 45
VOWELS ARE EMOTIONAL, CONSONANTS 46
    GIVE FACTS
WATER, WATER, EVERYWHERE 47
ARS POETICA 48
SELF PORTRAIT LETTERS 49

NOTES
ABOUT THE AUTHOR

For Hannah and Sasha

If there are any answers, I have lost them.
—Robert Frank

A Name for Everything

I. ALWAYS BEGIN WHERE YOU ARE

ALWAYS BEGIN WHERE YOU ARE

I'm not lost, I just don't recognize where I am.
—from the TV show, "Criminal Minds"

But anything worth doing, is worth doing badly.
— Jack Gilbert

Are dreams perhaps the soul's memories of the body and this
seemed a reasonable explanation.
—Jose Saramago, **The Gospel According to Jesus Christ**
translated by Giovanni Pontiero

DON'T WRITE yourself
into the between of words

prevail against
the meanings' multitude

trust the tear trace
and learn to live.

—Paul Celan, translated by Pierre Joris

SIN EATING

I was born with one eye open,
the caul, my inheritance.

Then day, night like failed logic.
Beyond questioning,

God may not appear.
Hard afternoon, thickened by flowers.

I wear my daughter's hat to hide

CARTOGRAPHY

The city was then three hands:
one missing two fingers, one drowning
in fresh buttons of dirt, one simply

not there. Unable to do anything else
with the stars they'd invented, someone
tossed them hard against the night.

It was a pale year of days at home,
orange cats, and dreams kept low
to the ground when we met.

Her face, violent and perfect
in any light, was everywhere. Any
window. I was nobody to stare at.

One slash and burn afternoon, we
stripped to make love and found
only bones made of light bulb glass.

Names, fat with dust, chatting
without regret about the weather
and the impossibility of money.

I'd live with my children in
a brick house but I've neither.
The houses invite no one and no one

is home. Soon the days will slip back
around my fingers, the doors will open
to any offer and there she'll be.

This is a map of everywhere we went.

THE MEMORY OF STARS

Streetlights mimic the caw-caw-
caw of stars pressed against
blackening skies. Another warm
night crawls across the Charles
where this afternoon sailboats
retraced the history of stars
falling to earth like dying angels
asking *What can I make for you* --
A teenage dream-car is trying
to barehand the asphalt from
the summer street. Two blocks
and thirty years earlier, it might
have been you. You remember her
smile, but not if you closed
your eyes when you kissed.
The last time you spoke, snow
was falling. Fifteen years
later, melancholy and drinking
alone, the sound of a car, angry
and in love reminds you of what
you forgot to ask. Do you really
believe those years littered
with headlights, dark houses
and middle-aged dreams were the best?
Like you, I've continued to live
where I can. To make up names
and towns for the years I don't
want to remember. Like you,
I still want only what's coming
to me to arrive one day after another.
To die every night until with eyes
opened and praying for light, morning
turns us back into our lives.

With the sun halfway down the back
of late afternoon, the first shirts,
ties and half-human voices
It's not about how you manage,

it's about how you make change
blaze sidewalks and streets
that flow like burned gold.
A saxophone player explains
how the world will end before
we get home. He'll play all day
and tomorrow and will die alone
in another winter, trying to
recapture the gray eyes,
angular smile and bruised heart
of the woman he dreamed was an angel.
Surrounded by their children,
their children's children,
the stillborn brothers and sisters
hold hands while three well-
mannered obsessions pray
over their names. Ghosts
in blue ties surround him
and unravel in an unbending
gaze of gray hair. Their child,
the one who could save the world,
sleeps in cardboard and snow.
His eyes bloody from wishing.

If despair, then not here.
The sun burns behind clouds
the color of broken teeth
and dreams of snow. Houses
lay like playing cards left
in the wind of hours no one
lives in. Behind our backs,
the wind insinuates the bus
will again arrive late.
There are mornings when I wonder
if this is where we've been
all our lives -- if this is
the only mirror our faces
look back from for memories.
All's quiet for now. Your letters
have grown small, less frequent

and remain in the hall closet
stacked among forty year old
magazines and family photographs,
in between two empty suits,
a close shave, crushed Stetson
and withered boutonniere.
The trees have become spider webs
of woven glass. The lights
are dying. Having stolen
from you everything I could,
save the dimness of your eyes,
I've come to remember your mistakes
were mine. Those are the mornings
when I awaken still strapped in
the driver's seat. Sunlight
pounding the dash. The world
I remember -- your voice,
a calm shirt over my chest;
your face in my pocket;
your hand covering my eyes
and your hand cold; the rustle
of your bones and everywhere
you ever took me -- falls apart
again. Nothing I could tell you
now will ever be big enough
for you to remember. It is
still winter. I'm waiting
in an over-priced hotel bar
for a glass of wine, a piano
trio and a woman who's brown
eyes are the color of salvation.
When the second set ends,
we'll return to separate houses,
cold and empty beds softened
by what's starry about darkness.

Before coming in, this night
paused at the window to sift
through the memories that litter
its pockets: an evening prayer

from the Himalayas, rain washing
over the lion-colored ankle grass
of the Serengeti, the noise gray
factory smoke from Detroit,
thirty-four species of tiger
lilies, a 19th century love letter
addressed to the imaginary saint
whose name I wear like a cheap suit,
the dreams of your whisper-thin
ghost whose paper heart pounds
against my life. I can hate you
no more than the lives that spill
between us like overheard conversations,
the bracelets of goose-like down
that covered your arms, the dim
storefronts and sidewalks that recite
your name. My thoughts mirror
the sin-eater's knife while it
crosses the corpse bread:
More air. More color. More light.
Think of something you never wanted
to discover beginning with how well
our clothes impersonate our lives.
I remain where you left off:
first light still hours away,
the house's breath shallow
and darkening. This is all I'll
ever remember: one day after
another rubbing the stars until
they collapse in the upstairs
bedroom of an abandoned house,
only to again rise from the dust
and bad luck of what they know,
again crossing the rivers and oceans,
tiptoeing over mountains, making
ladders of trees and birds' nests,
beating themselves perfect
and yellow against the sky.

A DESCRIPTIVE HISTORY OF MEMORY #1

Man. Rough skin pain grip. Smile-angry. Voice away, crawl—
clawed, tight-deeper. Noise, red-sharp noise
and more. Flip-flop sticky stick. Smile? Black
black blank. Water, scared water. Wash-away.
Hands smarter, more less pain. *It's ok* echo-splashing inside ears.

A DESCRIPTIVE HISTORY OF MEMORY #2

.

Night exhales cold escaping your overcoat.
Heaven's seven fixed stars at the window.
As if a mirror could animate shadows, give voices
uninflected reflections, terrified smooth flesh.
This prayer is for hell. I know it will find you

A DESCIRPTIVE HISTORY OF MEMORY #3

From the ash of his last cigarette, a frozen glass world.
Five, twelve, 47 years later,

miles, wood, dirt. As the dead should
be. Mute, x'd away. Thinking turned to worms.

Fooled light beckons rain, clouds in their unwashed overcoats.

A DESCIRPTIVE HISTORY OF MEMORY #4

Unhomed, voice drained
to hand-clotted syllables.

Door-light homewhere. Oh? Where?
Several worlds, look. Look how

noone isn't home. Never

A DESCIRPTIVE HISTORY OF MEMORY #5

Asleep in another uncombed field, dew-colored shirts,
graying flowers, rusted prayers. How loudly the dead

outweigh the living! Weary, wary of any
ever after, aching, wind-dead heartbeat.

Leaving hell and a one-way mirror for the living.

A DESCIRPTIVE HISTORY OF MEMORY #6

Sleep smartly, tight. Forgetting, of course,
the older ways. Blankets and sheets, curled back,

rising cold, windows feigning blind. The touch—
dreams, butterfly-splay softly, safely

white, warm, whispered into absence. But not.

A DESCIRPTIVE HISTORY OF MEMORY #7

How loudly the dead outweigh the living! Fragile,
carried ten or more aback, dew-colored shirts.

Asleep in another uncombed field.
Spike-grass, gray, flowers, prayer-rusted,

exquisite, overtired, wheezing-wakeful, here.

—————————

Good days wriggle, slither by
like unborn children. The bad ones,

hungry mouths caked with red dirt,
hang upside down, stabbed by light.

We are, none of us, born perfect.

A NAME FOR EVERYTHING

Dream-lit mornings startled
the days I never hoped for:

beginning with Chicago, later Detroit,
Charlotte, Boston, then again south

under thunderclouds weakened by light.
A prayer like ball lightning that once lit

on my hands before disappearing.
The last miracle of this century.

The blur from which again and again, I rise

II. FALLEN STARS
For Isabel

The vulnerability of precious things is beautiful because vulnerability
is a mark of existence.
—Simone Weil

Nothing begins without coming to an end, every beginning comes from an
ending.
—Jose Saramago, *The Gospel According to Jesus Christ*

Nothing is ever the same as they said it was. It's what I've never seen
before that I recognize.
—Diane Arbus

I can die now I just begun to live.
—Charles Olson, "Moonset, Gloucester, December 1, 1957,
1:58 A.M."

LOOKING FOR FALLING STARS, JULY 2006

City lights flatten against braided clouds.
Stretched against each other, breath whispering
to loved skin. It is a mild night, absent stars.
His arms imagine a falling star, the soft weight
of her legs and lips, fresh against him, a wish.

DREAMING IN FLESH, OF FLESH

As if he were to stand, eschew his frightened
wings, not argue air, or think windows deliberate
air. As if he could commiserate, spell God
and deliver what a pair of hands, lips, closing eyes
teach. Kiss and tell. As if every, any world in that moment.

SELF PORTRAIT WITH COFFEE

There is always coffee. The brown clink, aroma, and lighter
conversations. The possibility of history, beyond
nodding hair, the idea of smoke, whispering, caressed
paper. Watching her thinking. Her eyes. In some countries,
staring is indelicate intimacy. Hands feigning sight, blinking.

CONTEMPLATIVE, CURIOUS, THE BODY

A phrase of mind. Not blood and muscle, the heart.
Like skin, reunited, sewn, stapled, taped together,
almost again whole. If praying, I need to hear
my own voice, its transliteral borrowings
from God, to God, of God, for God, the blood-heart.

STUDY FOR FOUR HANDS

I would not hurt you ever. The grammar presupposes
a fortress: explains what isn't and cannot.

An evening shawl covers your shoulders,
wards off a cool breeze. Your eyes quiet away.

Candlelight breaching the near darkness
declining shadows. There is, as yet, nothing to suffer,

to photograph. A question he asked days ago still
leaves her naked. The words, in their pleasure

wonder what pleasure is and how. If she touches
his arm, then his hand. If he follows her eyes,

tenderly strokes her leg and traces her lips.
Other possible worlds, indiscrete gestures,

stubbornly, unlanguaged, ferocious. The economy
of feelings. Sans words, worlds.

Of what might record, settle, explain. And no.

PRAYER IN THE RAIN

If a star fell on top of your life, an untidy blessing
with arms, lips, eyes, and raw grace, words
become thoughtful accidents. There is no light,
there is no light, no unburned words, just ashes,
prayers to everything and how long it's been missing.

WEATHER REPORT

A day yawns on a face, pretending
to be another. Stretches across what
God meant to finish, like an albatross,
the bird God never intended. Chicago,
Detroit, Boston, Munich, Rome, then
harder west pretending to be ten days,
cards overturned on a table, faces and
numbers faded beige. This is where
I began. And once I get home,
somewhere close to the ground, with one
way out, I might sleep, look for food, re-
arrange the paper and books, uncurtain
the windows. If the sun is out, there
might be a breeze, another way to sleep
without poking dreams, a green scent.
I started out crawling, wound up upright
later, bent, and knotted whatever shape
my rage desired: cigarettes, bottle after
bottle of wine, vodka, bourbon, blood
throat screams, dented, broken objects
of affection, utility, necessity like un-clotted
air and water to disappear into. What became
of him or who, I don't know. A suit coat,
maybe, a nest of hair, something unkempt.
I think the door was open, so I came in.

A LOVELY QUICKNESS

July. Not a cruel month, but slothful. Heat tired.
What the window offers, that outside, is transparent,
luminous, impossible and to be held. Body-words,
worlds, expectant. A lovely quickness. A smile
of hair, food cooking. Sufferable, joyous light.

NOCTURNE

There is no higher compliment I can give you
than remembering your heart in my ear as we lay
under clouds whispering voyeuristically,
blushing in the dark, having forsaken beauty
for a moment's wind. It's wrong for you not to know
how beautiful you were in that moment before I lay
across you, geometry expressing the distance between
desiring and desire like the heart's two-word speech,
it's you it's you it's you it's you it's you. You should know
how your eyes softened, sending the guards home. How
what they know of what they won't tell is itself a night,
includes clouds, years walked down and thrown back.
What they carried slung across their back, silk-wrapped,
is the message I wanted to tell you, a red thread etched
on stone, a rune-script, a thin, crude scrawl, wakened.

MUSIC OF BROKEN LIGHTS

Warm, fictive, a breeze dusted room. How he imagines
her formal presence, a silk ripple, approximate skin,
its not touching. Brown-eyed. His, disconnected lightning,
errant, a feral blue air holds air, maybe colors. What
he would give, he would. The birds ignore him and sing anyway.

AN APOLOGY FROM ANOTHER SIDE OF THE OCEAN

The moon broadcasts its melancholic cure
for insomnia to houses darkened for sleep.
I left the door open. It has been decades
since a whisper, caressed shadow or loving
breath entered these rooms. Yesterday's
conversation was an angry child's whining
disappointment. I left a light on in the kitchen,
while you slept so your dreams might find me.
The stars exhausted all the music they know
accompanying the moon. By late afternoon,
I'll mistake how sunlight fills the room for a voice.
And pray if I hear them again, you'll answer.

LETTER TO TRIESTE

1.

Air, stuffed motionless, drained
of light. The rest is chaos. An alphabet.
If God were a painter, a conductor
of flowers, this would be the crescendo,
its opening strains. And always, always where she could be.

2.

Scars have names, finesse, education. Proud as water
wrestling a beach. To deny is, again,
to name, gain weight, decorate.
Color is useless. How much there is to know –
Rage, its cousins, how long to watch water before it boils.

3.

He would, she would, they would. Here is not
here. There is not there. So, neither is where either
is. Birds learned to fly, to explain fear,
renaming it air. Trees were an afterthought
like water, migration, cruelty. A flavor for all things.

III. LETTERS RESCUED FROM A FIRE
For g.

Faith is the power which permits us to believe what we know is untrue.
—Werner Herzog

We can imagine falsities, we can compose falsehoods, but only the
truth can be invented.
—John Ruskin

Writing letters is actually an intercourse with ghosts, and by no means
just with the ghost of the addressee, but also with one's own ghost,
which secretly evolves inside the letter one is writing.
—Kafka to Milena Jesenska

Because the moon was in my face the birds were blind
—Beckian Fritz Goldberg, from "I Have Lived Here All My Life"

SLOWDANCING WITH THE WOMAN IN RED SHOES

As she left, left him dark, near sleep, thinking he
might dream of her. He might, but
of red shoes conversing with a hallway,
passing listless coats,
unembraced and ready, aching for the cold.

PLAYING HOUE

Plastic fluorescence washes
the room. The red shoe,
a glass chair, the center
of the room. She leans against one wall.
His head against another. Silence
.
like an unopened window.
She picks up
the shoe, cradles it
before slipping it onto her foot
and putting the doll down again, already somewhere else.

DESIRE

Streetlights rest their hands
on his shoulders.

In shop windows, the world
repeating itself. Again he thinks

he hears her. And true or false
would do the same.

Icarus in mid-flight. His prayer.
The sun caressing his wings.

PARABLE

Living as he does making practical
monuments of his longings,
the voice pressed against the window
is tired and doesn't care about
a raincoat with a song in its pocket
or the lightning beneath his nails.
Thinks it's good to be alive
most days. The sun about there,
later maybe stars, unsuccessful lust,
remembered music. Pulls that room
from his pocket. Her heart, moon-lit,
slivered making its absence home.

VALENTINE

The heart is not real.
A muscle of its own making, necessarily unlovely,
insensitive to aesthetics. South Pacific cannibals believe
eating an enemy's warm heart offers
invincibility. What's true isn't always honest.

PRESENT

The present lies under the bed, wrapped,
ribboned, patient, as if intended
for God. *What can you know*, he whispers,
like a hand comforted by air just after being touched.
There is no mystery. The box is a box, empty.
And empty is as empty does

EVE OF SPRING

A month on, snow stars.
This night like another or next, lazy against the terrace.

Whatever remains is almost red, re-read, fondly
held. Not grace-touched.

His dog-tail heart,
beating against his ribs,

I'm here, I'm here, I'm here,
resuscitating the distance between hope and wisdom

like a bird's uneasy first flight.

BETWEEN FACT AND TRUTH

There is no light
beginning or ending the tunnel, no epiphenomenal

ball of lightning,
blessing praying hands.

He believes in what his fist
thinks, not in violence

but the *what if* of the window.
To see it, to understand requires going

through it. The wind bleeds past.
No one comes out alive,

drowning in the same river
twice, the same river,

the one beyond sight of a window, just.

ALWAYS BEGIN WHERE YOU ARE

A table, two cups, a large window sculpted
into an hour and a half conversation

disappearing into each word,
a twelve second embrace.

A postcard photograph of no one who was ever alive

STILL LIFE WITH DEAD BIRDS

A painted photograph of a woman un-sleeved in a white
silk dress, the necklace of hummingbirds

flittering noisy hearts restless
against her skin, shy of her breasts.

One hand holds a knife religiously; the other
empty, after holding conversation.

There is no face. No matter how the birds sing.

OCCASION

Dreams are accidents of birth.
—Barrett Watten, from "Plasma"

That existence. The moon, a night bird's evolving song, a yellowing
clock. He sleeps furtively, crumbled in his nest, misshapen books,
colorfully torn boxes, thudded cardboard colors, deepening,
loosened by the sun's choosing. The windows, both look
the same way, like his eyes, less inward, equally disheveled,
explained by rain-shadows, dust. If collected, his days would be
a time-collapsed photograph, a repetition of minute differences,
light clustered, inched, sullen and anonymous.... *please understand.*
His glasses, sculpted wire, stripped screws and glue holding
the lenses in place.

When I was a child, finally afforded that, the conflict of his two ages
becoming water. The birds, their songs, vapor trails. She, too, was
a child, frightened, articulate like Eurydice. Orpheus, her last
irritation, turned, turning, shrill. His plaintive song. Eurydice,
her wings, beginning and unnoticed as she turns home. Time
moving in both directions.

VOWELS ARE EMOTIONAL, CONSONANTS GIVE FACTS

The compromise between what he wants and what he wants.
A formula for happiness: yes, no, which.

WATER, WATER EVERYWHERE

.

Chinese poet Li Po is said to have died while drunk trying to
embrace the moon while it rested on the Yellow River. In March,
under several full moons and a series of hesitant rooms,
I discovered invisibility. Cried in spasms, the body comforting
itself, listening and hugging it like an empty coat, erasing sight,
body memory, the cold. That punctuation. Sometimes minutes,
sometimes hours. The river seduced a chaste moon, telling it
to whisper, explain joy, make it smile, wish and grow smaller.

ARS POETICA

We are named by all the things we will never understand.
　　—Amiri Baraka, (formerly LeRoi Jones) from
　　　"The Death of Horatio Algier"

The room lacks philosophy, sewn
as it is with chaste light, flirting

with walls, floor, corners, borrowed dust.
He is absent the way a hammer isn't an earring.

The room is what he wishes to be: not blind, blank,
monotonously breathing. The knock on the door

is mistaken. Wrong wrong wrong. It will
still be there if he returns. The weather

wears his clothes as always. The radio, trying to decide
between stations. That was last week, too.

SELF PORTRAIT: LETTERS

If thirty years equals one sentence
yes, I'm still walking: if by land, with

both eyes closed. If by water, sleepily.
These are the same shoes, socks

and untied laces. From here to back there
to here is harmless: small metal parts ground

precise, polished. Useless replacements.
It's that lonely time of year again,

hesitation all around like the wrong clothes
for a party. We used to speak, air passing

back and forth, a sailboat for questions,
rowboat for thoughts, fog like good luck.

Where were you? I was I, drowning knee deep,
hard of hearing and not uncertain this

wasn't hope, wasn't the promise I wanted.

NOTES

A Descriptive History of Memory is for Michael Ward. Some of the imagery in sections 5 and 7 is borrowed from the opening section of Charles Wrights' "Homage to Paul Cezanne"

Nocturne owes its shape and tone to Mark Cox's work. The line "It's wrong for you not to know how beautiful" is from "Running My Fingers Through My Beard on Bolton Road"

Desire is for Jack Gilbert and Linda Gregg.

Parable is for Jack Gilbert.

Between Fact And Truth is a statement made by Werner Herzog regarding his documentaries: "I am interested in the difference between fact and truth."

Vowels Are Emotional, Consonants Give Facts is a variation on a maxim of Nietzsche's taken from *Twilight of the Idols* (translated by Walter Kaufmann). "A formula for my happiness: a Yes, a No, a straight line, a *goal*."

ABOUT THE AUTHOR

Mark Fleckenstein was born in Chicago. Six states and dozens of moves later, he settled in Massachusetts. He graduated from University of North Carolina Charlotte with a B.A. in English, and Vermont College of Fine Arts with a MFA in Writing. He's been very involved in the poetry community in and around Boston, for over 30 years. He was an assistant editor for (BLuR), the *Boston Literary Review*, founder/coordinator of two bi-weekly poetry reading series in Boston and a workshop leader, He is also a painter. He has two amazing daughters and a large, eccentric, long-haired black cat named Ariadne.

www.ingramcontent.com/pod-product-compliance
Lightning Source LLC
Chambersburg PA
CBHW020218090426

42734CB00008B/1120